Things That
Make You Go
YUCK!

Ostriches

Things That Make You Go YUCK!

Extreme Living

Jenn Dlugos & Charlie Hatton

 Prufrock Press Inc.
Waco, Texas

Library of Congress Cataloging-in-Publication Data

Names: Dlugos, Jenn, author. | Hatton, Charlie, author.
Title: Things that make you go yuck! : extreme living/
  by Jenn Dlugos and Charlie Hatton.
Other titles: Extreme living
Description: Waco, Texas : Prufrock Press Inc., [2017]
  Audience: Ages 9-12. | Includes bibliographical references.
Identifiers: LCCN 2016035484 | ISBN 9781618215680 (pbk.)
Subjects: LCSH: Animals--Adaptation--Juvenile literature. | Animal
  ecology--Juvenile literature. | Adaptation (Biology)--Juvenile literature.
Classification: LCC QH546 .D5845 2017 | DDC 578.4--dc23
LC record available at https://lccn.loc.gov/2016035484

Copyright © 2017, Prufrock Press Inc.
Edited by Lacy Compton
Cover and layout design by Raquel Trevino

ISBN-13: 978-1-61821-568-0

Printed in the United States of America.

Prufrock Press Inc.
P.O. Box 8813
Waco, TX 76714-8813
Phone: (800) 998-2208
Fax: (800) 240-0333
http://www.prufrock.com

Giant Japanese
spider crab

Table
of Contents

Jumping spider

Introduction

Humans like to live on the edge. Skydiving, bungee jumping, eating the Chef's Surprise in the cafeteria—if there's a chance to push our bodies to the limit, we'll triple-dog-dare someone to do it. Centuries of human innovation have allowed us to survive—and thrive—in a wide range of environmental conditions. From airplanes that allow us to travel great distances in mere hours, to thermostats that regulate the temperature in our homes, humans are constantly figuring out new ways to live efficiently, comfortably, and most importantly, safely. In the wild, however, there are no emergency exits or remote-controlled air conditioners, so the simple act of survival often requires extreme biology.

The Extremes of Being

No matter if you consider yourself a daredevil or a cowardly lion, just hopping out of bed in the morning is proof that you live to the extreme. The human body is one of the most complex machines on Earth, containing an estimated 37 trillion microscopic parts called *cells*. These cells form tissues and organs that perform all of your life-sustaining functions in a quiet and efficient manner. (Unless you are in study hall. Then your body will perform its life-sustaining functions in a loud and embarrassing manner.)

Our organs also make up complex systems that are each dedicated to a specific life function. Your respiratory system fills you up with oxygen. Your nervous system allows you to respond to your environment. When you scarf down a juicy burger, your digestive system breaks it down into nutrients. But many organisms pooh-pooh our high-tech bodies. The simplest life forms on Earth are microscopic, one-celled organisms, which are capable of performing all the basic functions of life that our bodies require trillions of cells to do. No matter how normal you think you are, compared to some organisms, your very existence is the definition of living to the extreme.

HUMAN CELL

Lysosome Nucleus Nuclear membrane

Peroxisome

Chromosome

Mitochondrion

Cytoplasm

Golgi bodies

Cell membrane Endoplasmic reticulum Ribosomes

Boldly Going Where No Organism Has Gone Before

There are many ways to be extreme. Some of the organisms in this book are extremophiles, meaning they thrive in environments that are inhospitable to most forms of life. Extremophiles come in many different varieties. Thermophiles dig the sweltering heat. Psychrophiles crave Jack Frost's deep freeze. Others survive with virtually no water or oxygen. Simply put, if there's an environment capable of burning, freezing, or strangling other life forms, it's quite likely that some crazy creatures call it home sweet home.

Rebels With a Cause

The rest of the organisms in this book live in normal environments, but they have some characteristic that makes them stand out from the crowd. They are the mystifying misfits—they look weird, eat strange things, or have wacky behaviors that make everyone stop and point. Through genes, environment, or a combination of both, these one-of-a-kind oddities don't exactly blend in, which is fine by them. They are living proof that when survival is on the line, nature will very often lean to the extreme.

Grand Prismatic Spring

1 There's No Place Like These Homes

Some like it hot, some like it cold, and some like it virtually unlivable. This chapter is all about organisms that thrive in environments where few can even survive. From outrageous temperatures to toxic sludge, these inhospitable habitats are home to some of the hardiest organisms on Earth.

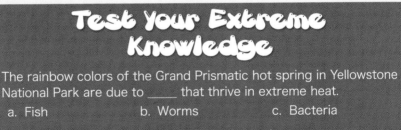

Test Your Extreme Knowledge

The rainbow colors of the Grand Prismatic hot spring in Yellowstone National Park are due to _____ that thrive in extreme heat.

a. Fish   b. Worms   c. Bacteria

Find out the answer at the end of the chapter!

Home Is Where the Heat Is

Nobody likes it when the house is too warm. It's hard to sleep, everything feels sticky, and all the ice cream melts. But there are animals out there that can live in levels of heat we humans never could. (Although we feel sorry for their cones of Rocky Road.)

On land, one of the most heat-loving—or thermophilic (thur-moe-FILL-ick)—species is the Saharan silver ant. They live in Africa's Sahara Desert, where sand temperatures can exceed 150 degrees Fahrenheit. To beat the heat, the ants are covered in tiny hairs shaped like prisms. These hairs reflect sunlight and heat, making the ants shimmer like silver, and keeping their body temperature low enough to survive—a comparatively chilly 128 degrees.

But Saharan ants can't hold a candle (or a blowtorch) to the animals who live life the hottest. Those are the Pompeii worms, which live near scalding hydrothermal vents deep in the ocean. Superhot gases leaking from under the sea floor heat the water above to more than 750 degrees Fahrenheit—too hot for any living thing. (Or for that matter, a well-done steak.)

Creatures do live near the vents, though, using the heat and nutrients to build thriving ecosystems. The Pompeii worms are among the bravest (and toastiest), living in tubes right next to the vents. Although the heads of the 4-inch-long worms usually rest in water around 72 degrees Fahrenheit, water inside the tubes where their backsides sit has been measured at 176 degrees. When Pompeii worms say, "It's like a sauna in here," they aren't kidding!

Best Friends in Fever

Like the Saharan ants, Pompeii worms use a clever trick to survive the heat. They team up with bacteria that form a thick fuzzy layer on the worms' bodies. The worms ooze a mucus that feeds the bacteria, and the bacteria are thought to insulate the worms against the heat.

Olly Olly Oxygen-Free

Most animals don't need much to survive—sunshine, fresh water, food, shelter, and air to breathe are a good start. But in 2010, scientists discovered animals who get by on far less.

Those animals are new species of *Loricifera* (lore-eh-SIFF-er-ah), tiny creatures less than a millimeter long that live in sediment on ocean floors all around the world. They look a bit like squids, only much smaller. A few dozen *Loricifera* species have been collected since they were discovered in the 1970s, but three found under the Mediterranean Sea turned out to be special.

That's because they were discovered in an area called the L'Atalante basin, which is extremely salty. Water at the bottom of the basin is 8 times saltier than other seawater, and doesn't mix with the water above. Because of this, there's almost no oxygen in the water either, and the waters are so deep and dense, no sunlight reaches the bottom. To top it off, toxic chemicals called *sulfides* are present there in high concentrations. The only life forms found to survive in such harsh conditions have been simple single-celled bacteria and archaea (are-KEY-uh).

And now, *Loricifera*. Scientists confirmed that the animals found in the sediment beneath the L'Atalante basin were living, molting, and reproducing—all without sunlight or oxygen, and surrounded by super-salty sediment and toxic chemicals. So much for the "comforts of home"!

Maybe They're Just Old-Fashioned

Besides taking the prize for "simple living," the *Loricifera* found under L'Atalante may help us understand animals from the distant past. Around 600 million years ago, the oceans held less oxygen and couldn't support large animal life—but perhaps early sea animals like *Loricifera* lived. By studying them, we might learn more about those prehistoric animals, too.

Pitch Your Tent in Pitch

A home on a lake sitting on a Caribbean island sounds pretty nice. And it probably is—unless the lake is Pitch Lake, in the town of La Brea on the island of Trinidad. That's because Pitch Lake isn't filled with water. Instead, it's filled with pitch, or liquid asphalt, which oozes up along with gases like carbon monoxide and methane from deep under the ground. In other words, Pitch Lake is a tar pit—in fact, the biggest in the world, holding 10 million tons of oozy asphalt.

That's not quite the island home we had in mind. But scientists have discovered organisms that manage to survive in the tarry muck. These single-celled creatures—

various species of bacteria and archaea—not only live in Pitch Lake, but eat there, too! Their meals consist of the tar and chemicals surrounding them. Not the tastiest tropical diet, we suppose—but the microorganisms don't seem to mind.

Besides the gooey neighborhood and nasty menu, the creatures in Pitch Lake face other obstacles that would stop most species cold. There's very little oxygen, for one thing, and also not much water. The critters manage to eke out a living inside tiny "microdroplets" of water, each about 1/20th the size of a raindrop. Still, the inhabitants seem to be doing okay—scientists estimate there are 1 to 10 million living cells in every gram of Pitch Lake asphalt. That sounds less like a tar pit, and more like a pool party. (But you might want to bring your own snacks.)

A Tar Afar?

Tar pits like Pitch Lake are fairly hard to find on Earth. But similar lakes, and even huge asphalt-like oceans, are common on Saturn's moon Titan. Finding living organisms in Pitch Lake has led scientists to wonder whether Titan could harbor life. Someday, we hope to find out.

Hobnob With a Blob

H umans excel at being couch potatoes. After all, we're the species that invented bean bag chairs, snooze buttons, and reality TV marathons. But humans may need to give up our comfy spot on the Slovenly Species' Sofa for the blobfish, a fish so lazy that it's nicknamed "The Couch Potato of the Sea."

The foul-faced blobfish is rarely seen by people, because it lives 4,000 feet under the ocean. Down there, the pressure is 120 times higher than it is at the surface. If you swam that deep without protection, your organs would crush into goo. But the blobfish finds it just peachy, because it actually *is* living goo. Most fish have swim bladders that fill with air and allow them to stay afloat. These fish can't live down with the blobfish, because the pressure would cause their bladders to swell and pop right out of their mouths (and you thought burping in the cafeteria was embarrassing). Instead of swim bladders, blobfish have light, jelly-filled bodies that allow them to float. They have soft bones and little muscle tone, so they can't even swim to find food. Instead, they just open their mouths and eat whatever swims, crawls, or scampers inside. For the blobfish, basically every day is Mystery Meat day in the cafeteria.

Not Exactly Photogenic

The blobfish was recently named the world's ugliest animal, but it's a bit unfair. Under the pressure of the deep ocean, it looks like a completely normal fish. It's only when it's pulled out of the water that it puffs out until it looks like a cranky uncle after Thanksgiving dinner.

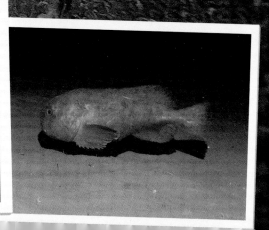

Enough to Make Your Blood Run Cold

Humans are pretty wimpy in cold weather. Before the temps drop to freezing, we dive under afghans and double-fist hot cocoa. But one little insect laughs at our chattering teeth and fuzzy socks. The red flat bark beetle lives in the unforgiving tundra of northern Canada. It has a distinctive red-hot color, but make no mistake—this bug is colder than ice. Recent research shows that adult flat bark beetles can survive temperatures as low as –72 degrees Fahrenheit.

These temps should freeze the beetles solid, but they have antifreeze substances in their bodies. When the cold hits, they purge as much water as possible from their bodies. This would be life-threatening for most organisms, but it's the only way these beetles can survive. Too much water increases the risk they'll freeze into a bugsicle. Losing water also boosts the concentration of the antifreeze substances in their bodies. (Think of it like iced tea. If you put too much water in, the tea tastes weak. If you use the same amount of tea but half as much water, it tastes stronger, because the tea has a higher concentration.) The dehydration and antifreeze create a perfect balance, allowing the beetles to survive some of the coldest temperatures on Earth. We just hope someone passes them a hot cocoa when spring comes. Brrrrr!

A Nip From Jack Frost

Without protection, humans can't survive for long in the conditions these beetles can. At −10 degrees Fahrenheit, with wind speeds of 5 mph, humans may experience frostbite after 30 minutes of exposure.

Extreme Knowledge Trivia Answer

The rainbow colors of the Grand Prismatic hot spring in Yellowstone National Park are due to _____ that thrive in extreme heat.

a. Fish
b. Worms
c. **Bacteria (Correct)**

Think About It

Research one of the planets in our solar system and the conditions that exist there. If you lived there, what type of home would you need to survive? How would you get food or survive the extreme temperatures? Could you safely walk around on the planet's surface, or would you need a special vehicle? Draw a picture of your new living quarters on your home-away-from-home planet!

This hot spring looks like a circular rainbow. Very few organisms live in the crystal blue center where the water temperatures reach 189 degrees Fahrenheit, but the green ring surrounding it houses plenty of heat-loving cyanobacteria. In fact, the cyanobacteria's ability to perform photosynthesis (the process that green plants use to make energy from the sun) gives the ring its green color. Similarly, the orange band surrounding the green is caused by bacteria that produce carotenoids. Carotenoids (cur-OUGHT-enn-oids) are yellow and orange pigments. These pigments give carrots and squash their orange color. A rust-red band along the outer edge is the coldest area of the spring. Many different microbes live here, and the pigments they produce give this ring its color.

2 Genes to the Extreme

Ever wonder why you have the facial features you do? Or how your body knew how to build all the organs you need to survive? The answer is in your genes, which are sections of DNA that code for traits and functions. Scientists study the DNA of different organisms to see how it's constructed. This chapter highlights some of the weirdest genomes they've found.

Test Your Extreme Knowledge

Frank and Louie was the name of a famous _____ that was born with two faces.

a. Cat   b. Dog   c. Fish

Find out the answer at the end of the chapter!

Back Off, Man!

I'm a GeneBuster

I f there's one thing in your body that needs a FRAGILE sticker, it's your genome. Your genome includes all of your DNA—including your genes—and it codes for every cell, organ, and tissue in your body. One organism, however, is really rough on its DNA. *Oxytricha trifallax* (ox-ee-TRICK-ah TRIFF-ah-lax) is a single-celled organism that shatters its genome into thousands of pieces and puts it back together just for self-improvement.

Most cells have one nucleus that acts like the cell's command center, but an *Oxytricha trifallax* organism has two. One nucleus keeps an intact version of its genome, and the other keeps a copy that's broken up into very tiny pieces. Oddly, the organism uses the messy nucleus to make the things it needs to stay alive while the neat-and-tidy DNA stays mostly untouched. Even stranger, it swaps DNA with other *Oxytricha trifallax* just to improve its own genome. When two *O. trifallax* swap DNA, they break it up, ditch some of their old genes for new ones, and build a new genome for themselves from the best pieces. (Imagine that you swap DNA with a friend, just so you can add some of his or her traits—like hair texture, skin color, or their one-of-a-kind facial features—to your own body. That's the level of sci-fi weirdness going on here.) These jigsaw masters reassemble thousands of fragments in just 2.5 days. We sure know who we're calling the next time we buy a LEGO kit.

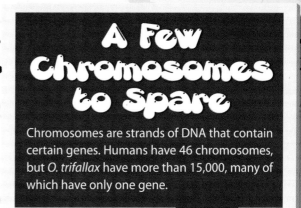

A Few Chromosomes to Spare

Chromosomes are strands of DNA that contain certain genes. Humans have 46 chromosomes, but *O. trifallax* have more than 15,000, many of which have only one gene.

Mite
You Give Me a Lift?

H ow many times do you hit the snooze button in the morning? Once? Twice? Enough times that you sprint to the school bus wearing one sneaker and one bunny slipper? If you need motivation to leap out of your bed in the morning, consider this yucky fact—you're probably sharing your mattress and pillow with thousands—likely millions—of tiny arachnids known as dust mites. Dust mites are microscopic, and some estimate that about 40,000 of them can live on a dust speck. They also dig travelling, which scientists discovered by taking a peek at their DNA.

DNA needs to copy itself when new cells are made, including sperm and egg cells that join together to form a new organism. Sometimes DNA makes a mistake during copying, which changes the genome. This is called a *gene mutation*. Mutations occur randomly, and some mutations—called *hereditary mutations*—can pass from parent to offspring. It is possible that a hereditary mutation may be common among a species living in one region and not found at all in a group of the exact same species living on the other side of the world.

Scientists found that dust mites in Pakistan and the United States—two countries located on different continents and separated by a huge ocean—shared a surprising amount of gene mutations, suggesting that dust mites are speedy international travelers. They spread their mutant selves from continent to continent, likely on our backs (and cars, trains, and boats). Given how many millions of them can cram into the average airplane, let's hope they at least stick to the two carry-on bags rule.

Home Sweet Cactus

If the thought of being around millions of mites grosses you out, you could always move to a place where your nearest neighbor is a cactus. Mites do not drink water—they absorb it through the humidity in the air—so they can't survive in extremely dry climates like deserts.

Skinny Genes

DNA is a bit like a school locker. At the start of the year, it's neat and orderly with everything in its proper place. By June, it looks like a Tetris puzzle, and you can't open the door without something falling on your head. Since the beginning of humankind, our DNA has accumulated a lot of "stuff." Some of this stuff is genes, which code for your traits. But most of it doesn't code for anything and scientists are not sure what current function—if any—most of these noncoding sections serve.

One plant makes a pretty compelling case for spring-cleaning the genome. The floating bladderwort plant is a carnivorous (meat-eating) plant that is a top-notch DNA editor. It has about the same number of genes as similar plants, but a much smaller genome, because it snipped out most of its noncoding DNA. Only 3% of its DNA is noncoding (for comparison, about 98% of human DNA is noncoding). No one knows why it became such an effective deleter, but scientists do have evidence that it duplicated its entire genome at least three times during its history—and edited it down to the short-but-sweet genome it has today.

Pass the Phosphorus

Floating bladderwort plants make their own energy from sunlight through photosynthesis, but they eat microorganisms for phosphorous, which is in low supply where they live. Plants need phosphorous to grow new tissue and use the energy they make from the sun. Most nonfloating plants get the phosphorous they need from the soil.

Yes, We Have Mutant Bananas

There are around 1,000 varieties of banana growing in the world, but there's a good chance you've only ever seen one. As it turns out, that's a big problem.

For every 100 bananas sold in stores, 95 are the Cavendish variety, the sweet yellow seedless fruit that most people know. Because the bananas have no seeds, they can't reproduce on their own. Instead, humans grow new trees from existing ones, which means nearly all the banana plants in the world have the same DNA. So when a disease threatens bananas, all the trees across the world face the same risk. If one Cavendish tree isn't immune, none of them are.

That's a real problem for banana growers. When a disease—usually a fungus—strikes one region, it can quickly spread to plantations all over the world. If the disease kills trees or develops resistance to treatments, it could potentially wipe out banana-dom as we know it.

Luckily, not all bananas are as genetically fragile. Other banana species are more resistant to disease—and scientists have tested inserting genes from those bananas into Cavendish bananas to make them resistant, too. Scientists have also looked for new mutations in Cavendish genes that make individual plants resistant. It may be possible to spread those mutations to other Cavendish bananas, making the whole variety stronger. That might sound crazy, but it's not. It's just bananas.

Playing Second Banana

A "banana catastrophe" has already happened. In the late 1800s, people enjoyed a variety called the Gros Michel, larger and sweeter than the Cavendish. But in the early 20th century, a condition called Panama disease nearly wiped the Gros Michel out. By the 1960s, the Cavendish, which happens to be resistant to Panama disease, was the main banana variety eaten worldwide.

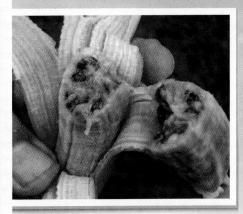

When You're a Shark, You're a Shark

When it comes to vertebrates—animals that have backbones—sharks are pretty unusual. They belong to a small group of fish, including skates and rays, whose skeletons are mostly made up of cartilage rather than bones. Within this group, the elephant shark (also called the elephant fish or Australian ghostshark) is even stranger, with a snout like an elephant's trunk that it uses to dig for food on the ocean floor. Elephant sharks probably get stared at a lot—but it turns out they've had a very long time to get used to it.

That's according to a team of scientists who sequenced the full genome of an elephant shark in 2014. By comparing the elephant shark DNA to DNA from other species, they found that elephant sharks are evolving more slowly than any other known vertebrate. That means the sharks' DNA isn't changing much over time. And because species similar to elephant sharks have been found in fossils more than 400 million years old, their DNA may not have changed much for an extremely long time. Slow and steady wins the shark race, we suppose.

Besides the slow evolution rate, studying the elephant shark's DNA has led to other discoveries. The scientists found that sharks are missing key genes needed to grow bones like most vertebrates, and also lack cells in the immune system that help higher animals—including humans—fight disease. Maybe those elephant sharks should hurry up and evolve already!

... But Not an Actual Shark

Despite the name, elephant sharks aren't technically part of the shark family, although they're closely related. Only three species of elephant shark exist today—including *Callorhinchus milii* (cal-low-RINK-us MILL-ee-aye), from which the DNA was sequenced.

Frank and Louie

Frank and Louie was the name of a famous _____ that was born with two faces.

a. **Cat (Correct)**
b. Dog
c. Fish

Many two-headed critters are actually conjoined twins, but Frank and Louie had diprosopus (dip-roh-SOP-us), a genetic mutation that gave him two faces at birth. Most cats with this condition live only a few days, but Frank and Louie was the oldest diprosopus cat on record. He was 15 years old when he died.

Think About It

In science fiction movies, a shape shifter is a person who can transform into someone else. Write a short story about a scientist who invents an extreme gene machine that changes a person's DNA, turning them into someone—or something—else.

Diving bell spider

3 Gross Anatomy

In a world where most of us try to fit into the crowd, some species know that weird is wonderful. The oddballs in this chapter certainly don't look like others of their kind, because they all have one, two, or 10 unconventional body parts that are sure to make you turn your head (or heads, if you have more than one).

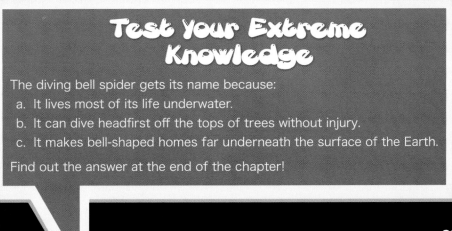

Test Your Extreme Knowledge

The diving bell spider gets its name because:

a. It lives most of its life underwater.

b. It can dive headfirst off the tops of trees without injury.

c. It makes bell-shaped homes far underneath the surface of the Earth.

Find out the answer at the end of the chapter!

It's All Fun(gi) and Games Until Somebody Bleeds

Even fungi need to floss. At least, some sure look like they do. If you trek far enough into the woods, you just may stumble across the gross and gooey bleeding tooth fungus. This fungus grows in big white clumps and drips a blood-red goop, which looks like Dracula dropped his dentures in the woods.

It's actually not the pearly white color that gives this fungus its fang-tastic name. It also grows tooth-like spikes underneath its hairy white caps. These spikes hold spores, allowing the fungus to reproduce. When the fungus is young and full of spores, its white cap spews a bright red liquid. When it grows old, the goop dries up, its cap turns brown, and all of its hairs fall out, making it look like a wrinkly old grandpa mushroom that's in bad need of a toupee.

So, are these fungi actually bleeding? No, but the red goop is still a bit of a mystery to scientists. It may protect the plant from germs, because it contains a substance that kills bacteria. It could also deter hungry critters from eating the fungi during reproduction. Despite the fungi's strawberries and cream appearance, the red goop has a disgustingly bitter taste that would put any cough medicine to shame.

Blood Buddies

Bleeding tooth fungi are often found growing on conifer trees (trees with cones). The fungus provides the tree with water and nutrients. In exchange, the tree gives the fungus a food supply.

Use Your
Heads

Think unicorns don't exist? Well, they do, but they're a wee bit smaller—and a lot scarier—than you'd expect. The larva of the *Uraba lugens* (oo-RAH-bah LOO-gens) moth is called the unicorn of caterpillars due to the ginormous horn on top of its head. The scary part is that it doesn't grow its horn—it makes it out of its old heads.

Caterpillars have hard exoskeletons that can't grow, so they need to shed them occasionally through a process called *molting*. Many molting critters simply discard their exoskeletons, but this little caterpillar keeps one part—its old head. From molt to molt, it piles up its discarded heads, eventually building a giant stack-o-skulls that forms a horn. Scientists don't really know how the horn stays together, but the caterpillar's fuzzy hairs may help tie it on.

These horns seem to give the caterpillars a heads-up—pun intended—on survival. Researchers observed that predators often attacked the horn instead of the caterpillar, which may give the caterpillar a chance at an escape. Another study found that in a mixed group, horned caterpillars were more likely to survive than those without horns. More research is needed, but there is no doubt that for these caterpillars, it pays not to lose their heads.

A Skeleton With Many Skulls

Uraba lugens caterpillars are called *gum-leaf skeletonisers*, but the name does not come from their unusual headwear. They are quite destructive to Eucalyptus plants, eating everything but the veins of the leaves, leaving the plants looking like bare, green skeletons.

I Only Have
Bubble Eyes
for You

There are a few things we've come to expect from pet goldfish. They swim. They eat. They refuse to go into that cool aquarium castle you spent your entire allowance to buy. We certainly don't expect that our little pet goldfish will do something unexpected, like sprouting giant bubbles for eyes, but for one type of goldfish, that is just a normal day.

Bubble-eye goldfish are born looking relatively normal, but eventually their eyes actually pop out of their head. Due to a deformity, they grow two giant, fluid-filled bubbles around their eyes that force their eyes upward, limiting their range of vision. The bubbles are quite fragile—just one sharp aquarium pebble can pop one, which can sometimes cause a serious infection. Often, a bubble will grow back, but it can grow to be a completely different size than the original bubble, turning the poor little bubble-eye into a lopsided fish.

Carting around two giant bubbles would slow down anyone's swim speed, but these fish also have a big steering problem. They usually lack a back fin, which helps fish make smooth turns and stay upright. Owners of bubble-eye goldfish often keep them separated from faster fish, because the speedy fish will eat all the food before the clumsy bubble fish can fumble his way to dinner.

Eye See You

Scientists use goldfish to study human vision, because their eyes see the same colors we do. In fact, they have even better vision. Their eyes have a receptor that we do not have, which allows them to detect ultraviolet light.

Eight-Legged Assassins

Spiders have some pretty freaky anatomy, what with the eight legs and eight eyes and shooting silk out their butts. But it could be worse—for instance, be glad that spiders don't also have long giraffe necks and huge pincers with poison fangs. Except for the spiders that do.

Those so-called assassin spiders come from the *Archaeidae* (are-CAY-eh-day) family, which live in Australia, Madagascar, and South Africa. These eight-legged oddballs have heads perched atop long skinny necks, nearly the lengths of their bodies. And sticking out of their faces, beneath those eight spidery peepers, are enormous pairs of jaws, just as long as their necks. At rest, the jaws droop down in front of the body, like

40

the bill of a large bird. In fact, some people call them *pelican spiders*. But they behave in ways we're pretty sure pelicans don't.

For starters, assassin spiders mostly walk upside down, on the undersides of leaves. With their gangly necks and jaws, it's actually harder for them to walk right-side up. Also, they survive by eating other spiders—hence the "assassin" name. Assassin spiders creep slowly up to another spider's web, and pluck the web with their legs. When the other spider investigates, the assassin spider extends its jaws and grabs it. Tiny fangs at the jaws' tips inject venom into the victim, while the jaws keep the prey a safe distance away, in case it tries to bite back. It sounds more like a "ninja poison giraffe spider" to us, but we figure this thing has enough names as it is.

You've Got Something on Your Face

Technically, assassin spider "necks" aren't really necks—they're more like stretched-out faces. That's because the spiders' mouths are actually below the neck and not on the face above. When the spiders feed, their pincers droop back down, bringing food right to the mouth. Yum?

One "Powerful" Flower

Most plants need insects for pollination to grow flowers. Most plants also grow leaves and branches, and use photosynthesis to store energy from sunlight.

Hydnora africana (hid-NOR-ah aff-ree-CON-ah) is a plant native to southern Africa—but it's not like most plants. For starters, *Hydnora africana* doesn't grow leaves or twigs or produce chlorophyll for photosynthesis. The plant is just a tangle of underground roots, a fruit (also underground), and a flower. The flower is connected directly to the roots, and just the tip breaks through above the ground. And what a flower it is.

Hydnora africana flowers look like alien pods, and smell worse. Each one has three scaly-looking flaps connected with white fibers. Over time, the fibers unravel and the "pod" opens up, like a nightmare from *Little Shop of Horrors*. All the while, the flower reeks of dung. It's not likely to unseat the rose as the go-to Valentine's Day bloom, is what we're saying.

This nastiness does serve a purpose, however. *Hydnora africana* depends on dung beetles to carry pollen from one flower to another, helping the plants to reproduce. By smelling like dung, the flowers attract the beetles to climb through the fibers for a meal. The beetles are trapped for a while—the better to pick up more pollen—before the flowers open up to release them. If the plants are lucky, those beetles will crawl into another flower and deliver the pollen.

The Root-Sucker of All Evil?

Although *Hydnora africana* plants are nice to their beetle friends, who get free meals while they're stuck inside, their other neighbors don't fare as well. *Hydnora africana* is a parasite that attaches to the roots of nearby plants and sucks needed nutrients away from them.

43

Diving bell spider

The diving bell spider gets its name because:

a.   **It lives most of its life underwater. (Correct)**
b.   It can dive headfirst off trees without injury.
c.   It makes bell-shaped homes far underneath the surface of the Earth.

If you think you'll never meet a spider when swimming, think again. The bell spider lives almost its entire life underwater, because it constructs an air web that allows it to breathe. One research study found that these spiders com surface as little as once a day for fresh air.

Think About It

All animals have specialized body parts that help them to survive in their environment. These parts can help them catch food, run from predators, regulate their body temperature, or perform other functions. Think of two animals—one that lives in a very cold climate and one that lives in a very hot climate. What body parts do they have that help them survive in their habitats? Could each one survive in the other's habitat? Why or why not?

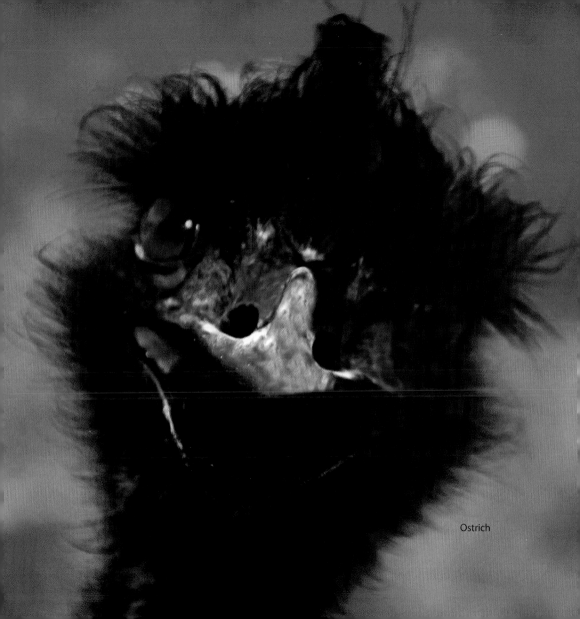

Ostrich

4 Supersize Species

You probably have an idea about how large most species grow—and you're likely mostly right. You won't see hornets as big as fighter jets, or a rabbit the size of a Volkswagen. But once in a while, nature whips up an exception—an organism way, way bigger than anyone would expect it to be. In this chapter, we crane our necks upward to check out these "supersize species."

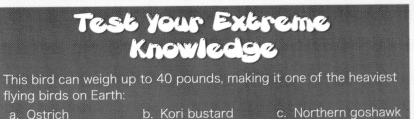

Test Your Extreme Knowledge

This bird can weigh up to 40 pounds, making it one of the heaviest flying birds on Earth:

a. Ostrich   b. Kori bustard   c. Northern goshawk

Find out the answer at the end of the chapter!

Two's Company, This Tree's a Crowd

There are some awfully big trees out there. California's giant sequoias, for instance, are famously huge—and hugely famous. A single sequoia can span 100 feet around the trunk, live for 3,000 years, and weigh 3–4 million pounds! Those numbers might put your neighborhood oak or dogwood to shame—but they're not the biggest among all trees. Not even close.

So which tree species makes sequoias look like bonsais? That would be the quaking aspen, *Populus tremuloides* (pop-YOU-luss trim-you-LOY-dees). The tree gets its name because its leaves rustle easily in the wind, giving the impression the whole tree is trembling. But it's not afraid of something bigger—because among creatures now living on the planet, nothing else is.

Aspens don't grow as single trees, but sprout from an interconnected underground root system. An entire forest of aspen trees may actually be one organism, with each tree a genetically identical copy or "clone" of the others. The largest known aspen growth is a grove in Utah called "Pando," with around 47,000 connected trees. It spans 107 acres (bigger than Disneyland!), weighs about 13 million pounds, and may be 80,000 to one million years old.

Sorry, sequoias. If you want to outgrow these aspens, you've got a lot of work to do.

A More Humungous Fungus?

Although quaking aspens take the prize for heaviest living creatures, they don't quite make the grade for biggest, in terms of area. That honor belongs to a parasitic "honey fungus" from the species *Armillaria* (arm-ill-AIR-ee-uh), which causes root disease in trees across the U.S. and Canada. One patch of interconnected, mostly underground fungus discovered in Oregon covers nearly 2,400 acres—almost 4 square miles, or the area of 1,665 football fields.

Breaking the (Slime) Mold

C ells are the building blocks of life. Some organisms, like bacteria, have just one cell. Others, like violets and vultures and Venezuelan poodle moths, are built from many cells. There are trillions of cells inside your body—more than the number of galaxies in the known universe!

Of course, to pack all those cells into one person—or flower, or bird, or poodle moth—the cells have to be very small. Whether alone or connected in a large organism, each individual cell is microscopic, invisible to the naked eye. Unless that cell is a certain type of slime mold.

Slime molds begin life as tiny single cells, like many other unicellular critters. They eat bacteria and other microbes, are often found in forests on rotting logs or dead leaves, and can gather together into a mass to find food or prepare to reproduce. But one type, called *plasmodial* (plaz-MOE-dee-ull) *slime molds*, takes this togetherness to a whole new level.

Like most species, these molds make a new copy of their genetic material, or DNA, as they grow. Usually, cells do this just before dividing into two new cells, each of which gets its own DNA copy. But a plasmodial slime mold cell doesn't divide. Instead, it keeps copying its DNA over and over, growing larger and larger, until one single cell has hundreds or thousands of copies of genetic material. That cell can be a foot wide or more—easily seen with the naked eye.

A Master Among Molds

One mold species, *Physarum polycephalum* (fie-SARE-um paul-ee-SEFF-ah-lum), has been studied by scientists for decades. Incredibly, the mega-sized single-celled critter has demonstrated a knack for intelligent behavior in the lab, showing signs of memory, problem solving, decision making, and anticipating environmental changes. Now that's one smart slime.

Shoo, Fly,

Shoo!

Most people have dealt with houseflies. They buzz around and walk on your picnic potato salad, but (apart from the diseases they may carry) are fairly harmless. If you live near woods, a beach, or in an area that stays warm most of the year, you may also run into houseflies' bloodthirsty biting cousins, like deer flies, horse-flies, black flies, or sandflies. Ouch.

Luckily, these bloodsucking bugs aren't as large as the biggest flies we know of. Those would be members of the mydas and timber fly families, which live in South and

Central America. The heat must be good for their health, because these flies grow up to be monsters.

Among mydas flies, the species *Gauromydas heros* (gar-ooh-MY-das HEE-ros) is the biggest of all. Although little is known about the species' life cycle or behavior, specimens have been found measuring 6–7 centimeters long, with wingspans up to 9 centimeters, or about the length of a crayon! Timber flies are about the same size, reaching 8 centimeters in length, with wingspans about the same. If one of these flies bit you, you'd feel it!

Luckily, neither kind of these formidable flies is likely to bite. Besides living in remote tropical habitats, these insects have pretty tame menus. Mydas flies are thought to feed on flower nectar, and adult timber flies don't have fully developed mouths. They don't live very long, and may not eat at all. The flies in our neighborhood could learn a thing or two from them!

Not a Fly, But Oh My!

While mydas and timber flies are the largest of the "true" flies, scientifically speaking, there are other—and bigger—flying insects out there. In 2014, a giant dobsonfly specimen was collected in China with a wingspan of 21 centimeters—longer than a hot dog bun!

Getting the Short End of the Stick

Located between Australia and New Zealand, Lord Howe Island was home to incredible giants. Lord Howe stick insects grew up to 5 inches in length, large enough that locals called them tree lobsters and used them as bait to catch larger fish. In the early 1900s, a ship carrying stowaway rats came to the island. The rats quickly developed a taste for the giant stick insects, and the insects' population plummeted. In 1960, the bug giants were declared officially extinct.

Then something very strange happened. About 12 miles away from Lord Howe Island is Ball's Pyramid, the remains of an old volcano. Climbers of Ball's Pyramid reported seeing bodies of the long-extinct stick insects. In 2001, a group of scientists made the treacherous climb to see if they could find evidence that the insects still existed. They were stunned to find a total of 24 giant stick insects—as healthy as could be—crawling around the volcano. After an extensive search of the Pyramid, they concluded that these were the only 24 individuals left in existence. After 2 years of pleading their case, the scientists were eventually permitted to remove two breeding pairs of these insects from the wild to mate them. One of the places that received a pair of insects was the Melbourne Zoo in Australia. By 2016, the zoo hatched 13,000 giant stick insects, and the number continues to grow.

Dirty Rats

Although there was a happy ending for the giant stick insects, not all species on Lord Howe Island had one. The rats drove 12 other species of invertebrates on the island to extinction.

The World's
Largest Claw
Machine

If you're scared of spiders, you don't want to dive too deep into the waters around Japan. Although there are no actual spiders down there, there is a critter that looks like an arachnophobe's worst nightmare. The Japanese spider crab has eight long legs that reach a leg span of up to 13 feet—about the length of a car—and two sharp claws. They are the largest crabs on Earth.

Japanese spider crabs can live very long lives—up to 100 years, scientists estimate— but they certainly don't age gracefully. Their long, skinny legs are quite fragile. A group of researchers discovered that the majority of the crabs they studied in one particular region were missing at least one limb, most commonly one of the two front walking legs. Fortunately, almost all the missing limbs were legs and not claws, which the crab relies on for defense.

Due to their size, the largest spider crabs have few predators, but younger and smaller crabs can be easy pickings for hungry sea creatures. To protect themselves, smaller crabs cover themselves with algae, kelp, and other sea matter to camouflage themselves.

The Biggest Entrée Ever

Spider crabs live in ocean depths up to 2,000 feet, but they move to shallower waters to reproduce. These crabs are actually a delicacy in Japan, but to help maintain their population size, it's against the law for fishermen to catch them when they are in these shallower, and more accessible, waters.

Kori bustard

Extreme Knowledge Trivia Answer

This bird can weigh up to 40 pounds, making it one of the heaviest flying birds on Earth.

- a. Ostrich
- **b. Kori bustard (Correct)**
- c. Northern goshawk

Kori bustards are native to Africa, and the females are about half the size of the males. Males on average weigh about 30 pounds, but they can reach up to 40 pounds. Due to their extreme size, these birds are not particularly keen on flying, but they will when necessary. Their long legs and three-toed feet are better equipped for running, so they'll often run to get away from predators.

Think About It

Imagine that you are shrunk down to the size of a bug. If you went outside, what type of gigantic critters would you come in contact with? What type of home would you build to survive? Draw a picture of your "mini-you" surrounded by all the giant critters in your neighborhood!

Earthworms

5 Eat, Drink, and Be Scary

Most of us have at least one weird food habit. Do you eat your cake layer by layer? Chop the crusts off your sandwich bread? Gag when foods touch each other on the plate? No matter how strange your snacking habits are, you can't hold a spork to some of the finicky feasters in the wild. From disgusting diets to bizarre meal preparation rituals, these animals definitely earn the title of extreme eaters.

Test Your Extreme Knowledge

This simple animal tears open a new mouth hole every time it eats.

a. Hydra   b. Sea star   c. Earthworm

Find out the answer at the end of the chapter!

The Spider Catches the . . . Acacia?

Spiders are made to kill. They have huge fangs, paralyzing venom, and the ability to wrap their victims up in a silk burrito. It has long been assumed that all spiders are primarily meat eaters, until scientists found one little Mexican spider that says "no thanks" to food with a face.

Spiders feed mostly on insects and small animals, but a few rare species have been spotted chowing down on nectar, pollen, and other plant parts. Most of these plant-eating spiders are jumping spiders, including a species named *Bagheera kiplingi* (bag-HEE-rah kip-LING-ee). For *Bagheera kiplingi*, plants aren't just a rare treat. Nearly its entire diet is plant-based, making it the first primarily vegetarian spider ever discovered.

Because jumping spiders do not build webs to trap food, *Bagheera kiplingi* may have developed a taste for plants simply because plants are easy meals. Parts of acacia trees make up the bulk of this little spider's diet, but it does occasionally eat small flies or ant larvae. Toward adult ants, however, *Bagheera kiplingi* has a bad case of ant-a-phobia. Acacia plants are protected by a particularly aggressive ant species that will not hesitate to swarm, kill, and devour a plant-eating spider. But *Bagheera kiplingi* has figured out how to jump from meal to meal with precise timing to avoid being spotted by the killer ants. It uses similar techniques that other jumping spiders use to hunt, except instead of catching a yummy bug, *Bagheera kiplingi* uses its killer instincts to hunt down a spider-ific side salad.

The Eight Eyes Have It

Jumping spiders have the sharpest vision of all spider species. They have four large eyes that give them sharp central vision, and four smaller eyes that give them side vision.

63

A Bare-Bones Diet

Some folks have acid tongues, and their nasty comments cut you to the bone. Others just smear acid on your bones and eat right through them. *Osedax* worms fit into the second category. Despite having no teeth or mouths, these worms survive by chowing down on the bones of massive ocean animals.

Osedax worms were first discovered in 2002 in Monterey Bay, CA, and it didn't take long for scientists to realize how weird they are. The females are 1–3 inches in length, but the males are microscopic. Dozens, even hundreds, of males live inside a tube that surrounds a female worm. Only females eat bones, but scientists are still not sure exactly how. These worms lack teeth, a mouth, and a stomach, so how do they even eat in the first place?

Researchers did find that these worms have a bone-melting acid on their skin. They also have roots that contain beneficial bacteria, which likely help the worms digest nutrients from the bone. Scientists aren't exactly sure how the nutrients get from the bacteria to the worms— the worms may consume the bacteria or the bacteria transfer it some other way. No matter how it's done, it sure is effective. Some worm colonies consume an entire whale skeleton in only a few years.

Which One of You Ate My Fossil?

Osedax worms—or close relatives—have likely been around for millions of years. New research found holes in plesiosaur bones (an extinct aquatic reptile) that matched the holes modern *Osedax* worms make in whale bones.

The Shish Ke-Bird

Meat on a stick. It's a staple of county fairs, family barbeques, and anywhere else pesky forks and knives get in the way of chowing down your grub. Since there aren't a lot of utensil dispensers in the wild, one little bird makes do by eating its prey shish kebab style.

Shrikes are small—and deceptively adorable—birds, but a few varieties have a sinister side. They eat mostly insects, mice, lizards, and other small prey, but once they've captured their meal, they carry it to the nearest thorn or suitably sharp object and skewer it, making instant meat-on-a-stick meals. This strange—and quite gross—habit has a few perks for the birds. It allows them to anchor their meal, so they can really dig in. It also gives them a way to store their food for later. It's not uncommon for shrikes to leave their kills skewered for days, which is especially beneficial when they've caught a poisonous critter. Some shrikes are known for eating toxic grasshoppers. The grasshopper's poison would kill most predators, but the shrikes keep their grasshoppers on the spikes for a few days, which dries up the poison, making them safe to eat. Stocking up the pantry with pierced prey also comes in handy during mating season, and male birds will often decorate their skewered meals with feathers to attract their mate. It's nice to know that in the shrike world, romance isn't dead—it's just a bit skewered.

Five Pounds of Field Mice, Please

Shrikes are appropriately nicknamed "butcherbirds," because their meals look similar to slabs of meat hanging on meat hooks in a butcher's freezer.

I Want to Suck Your Brood

Being young is hard. Kids have to put up with a lot of things from adults. But better to be a human kid than a young ant of the species *Adetomyrma venatrix* (ah-debt-oh-MURR-mah VENN-ah-tricks), or "Dracula ant." Yes, Dracula ant. You can probably see where this is going.

Dracula ants live on the island of Madagascar, and were only discovered in the 1990s. The ants are blind and have abdomens that resemble wasps, from which ants are thought to have evolved around 80 million years ago. Adult Dracula ants may be workers (without wings), drones (males with wings), or queens (females that can lay eggs). None of these adults can eat solid food—but the young larval ants can. That's where the "Dracula" part comes in.

Dracula ant workers use long venomous stingers to stun other insects. They bring the prey back to the nest for the larvae to feed on—but that doesn't help the adults. To get their meals, they scratch and bite at the larvae's backs until they "bleed," and suck down the fluid.

(Ants have fluid in their bodies called *hemolymph* [HEE-mow-lymph], similar to the blood found in humans and higher animals. It's this hemolymph that Dracula ants feed on.)

The feeding process has been called *nondestructive cannibalism*, because the young larval ants survive the experience. But they don't like it much. Scientists have reported that when adult Dracula ants enter the chamber, the larvae try to run away. We don't blame them one bit.

Fancy Antsies

Because of their resemblance to wasps and other characteristics, Dracula ants are thought to be a "missing link" between the two types of insects. Scientists hope to study the species further, but they may have to hurry— Dracula ants are currently a critically endangered species.

The Olm-ost Perfect Diet

S ometimes, the most impressive thing an organism can eat is nothing at all. You've probably heard about bears that eat nothing for weeks while they hibernate, or camels managing without food and water for a month, or crocodiles waiting a year or more between meals. But did you know there's an animal that can go without food for more than a decade? Now that's some serious dieting willpower!

This rarely ravenous animal is called the olm (species *Proteus anguinus*, or PRO-tee-us ang-WEE-nus), and there are plenty of strange things about it besides its menu choices. The olm is a type of salamander that lives in water flowing through underground caves in Slovenia, Croatia, and other areas near the Adriatic Sea. It's the only fully cave-dwelling vertebrate in all of Europe, and lives in complete darkness underground—which is just as well, as olms' eyes don't fully develop, so they're completely blind. For creatures their size—about a foot in length—olms live a very long time, 60 years or more on average, with some living more than 100 years!

As for their eating habits, olms swallow crabs, snails, and insects whole, but when no food is available, they don't make a fuss. A research scientist kept one olm in water in a refrigerator for 12 years without any food. By the end, the olm had lost a lot of weight, and even broken down some of its internal organs, but it was still alive. And was hopefully rewarded with a big snack. Even the most serious dieter should get to "cheat" every decade or so.

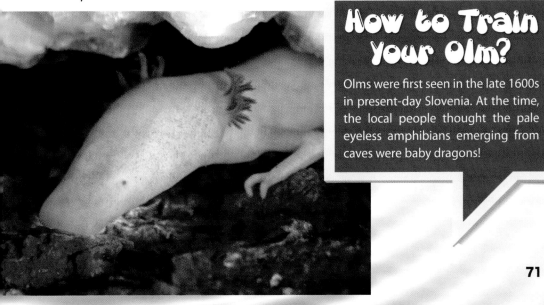

How to Train your Olm?

Olms were first seen in the late 1600s in present-day Slovenia. At the time, the local people thought the pale eyeless amphibians emerging from caves were baby dragons!

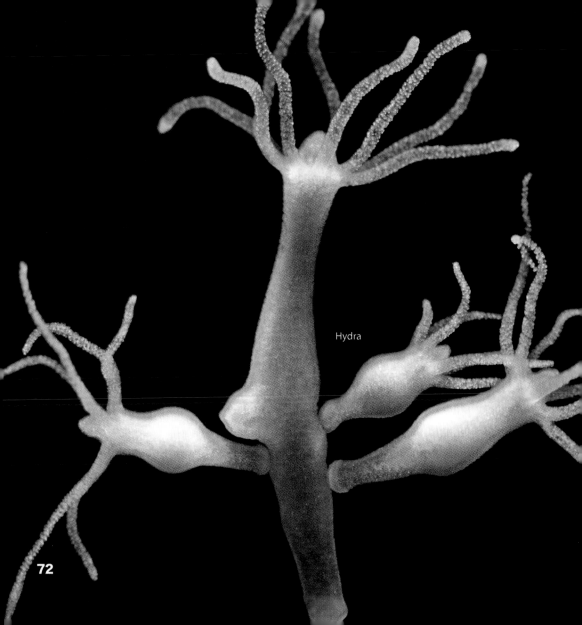

Hydra

Extreme Knowledge Trivia Answer

This simple animal tears open a new mouth hole every time it eats.

a. **Hydra (Correct)**
a. Sea star
b. Earthworm

These tentacle-wielding animals may be tiny, but their incredible ability to regenerate makes them the superheroes of the sea. If you cut a hydra in half, each piece will grow back its missing parts to form a whole new hydra. A group of scientists recently studied one type of hydra and learned that it did not have a permanent mouth opening. Instead, it tore open a new mouth every time it ate by stretching and separating its skin cells.

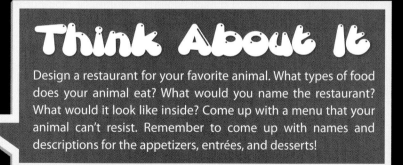

Think About It

Design a restaurant for your favorite animal. What types of food does your animal eat? What would you name the restaurant? What would it look like inside? Come up with a menu that your animal can't resist. Remember to come up with names and descriptions for the appetizers, entrées, and desserts!

Snowshoe hare

6 Death Defiers

It's a dangerous world out there. Any number of grisly fates could befall a careless organism, from freezing to burning to drowning to drying out to suffocating to being shot into the depths of space. (Granted, some of these scenarios may be more likely than others.) These are deadly situations for just about any species—except the ones in this chapter, who have learned how to cheat death and survive some of nature's scariest predicaments.

Test Your Extreme Knowledge

This animal can survive the winter months with 2/3 of the water in its body completely frozen.

  a. Wood frog   b. Snowshoe hare   c. Chinook salmon

Find out the answer at the end of the chapter!

Who's Jealous
of a Jellyfish?

You can't stay young forever. People have tried—from Ponce de Leon to Peter
Pan to Dorian Gray. It didn't work out so well for them. But then, none of
those people were jellyfish.

Specifically, none of them belonged to the jellyfish species *Turritopsis
dohrnii* (turr-ee-TOP-sis DOOR-knee-aye). Members of this species don't stay young
forever, either—but they have an even better trick. They can revert back to youth, over
and over again. Barring an accident (or being eaten by some sea creature), this basically
makes the jellyfish immortal.

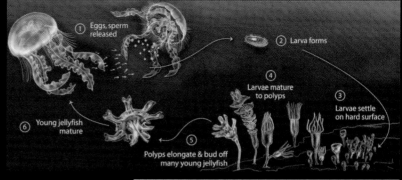

① Eggs, sperm released
② Larva forms
③ Larvae settle on hard surface
④ Larvae mature to polyps
⑤ Polyps elongate & bud off many young jellyfish
⑥ Young jellyfish mature

Turritopsis jellyfish start life as other jellyfish do, in a larval form. These tiny swimmers don't look like jellyfish yet, and eventually settle on the ocean floor, where they form polyps. The polyps bud off and grow into the "medusa" form we think of as jellyfish, with a round dome atop a mass of floating tentacles. Many jellyfish species go through a similar life cycle.

But *Turritopsis* medusas take the "cycle" part of "life cycle" very seriously. When faced with a crisis—like physical damage or lack of food—these jellyfish don't lie down and die, or throw up their

Globetrotting Jelly

Turritopsis jellyfish only pull the revert-to-childhood trick in case of emergency, and individuals do die. Still, as a species, their clever strategy seems to be successful. Scientists report that these "immortal" jellyfish are spreading throughout the oceans in large numbers.

tentacles in despair. Instead, they shed those tentacles, change the way their cells grow and behave, and grow into an un-jelly-like ball of cells called a *cyst*. This cyst can then form polyps from which new medusas can grow. The jellyfish never die; they just enjoy a second childhood. And a third, and so on. Just imagine all the hand-me-downs they must go through.

Mummified
Mosses

Every species on Earth needs water to survive. Besides the water that animals drink and plants soak up from rain, most creatures are made up more of water than of anything else. You're roughly 70% water, in fact. Or slightly more, if you just had a big glass before bedtime.

Because water is so important, it's bad news when an organism dries out—or *desiccates*, as the process is called. Losing water affects a creature's shape, keeps nutrients and proteins from flowing where needed, and disrupts nearly every function of living cells. Although some species (like camels) can go a long time without taking in more water,

losing the water they've stored up is another story. Most species can't survive severe desiccation. But star moss can.

The star moss *Tortula ruralis* (tore-TWO-lah roo-RALL-iss) looks like other mosses most of the time. It grows bright green stems and leaves, and lives in nearly every type of climate. But when water grows scarce, the moss does something unique—it produces proteins that can repair the damage of losing all the water, along with others that will detect when water is available again and bring the moss back to life. Then the moss shuts down and becomes dormant.

A moss can survive in this dormant state for a long time—70 years or more!—without dying, because it doesn't require energy. Once the water returns, though, the moss springs back to life, unfurling leaves within seconds. That's why some call these mosses "resurrection plants."

When In Drought, Moss It Out!

Tortula's desiccation-resistance powers may someday help others, too. Scientists are studying the moss to understand how it survives without water, and whether other plants could do the same. This could save many crops and other important plants in times of severe drought.

To Kill a
Tardigrade

Tardigrades (TAR-duh-grades), as you might guess from their other common names, "waterbear" and "moss piglet," are awfully cute. They're tiny animals, about the size of that comma back there, and they do resemble tiny stout (eight-legged) bears or pigs. There are more than 1,000 species of tardigrades known, and they live all over the planet in just about every type of habitat. Adorable, fascinating, and scientifically useful, we can't imagine any reason to kill one.

Which is good. Because it's darned near impossible to kill a tardigrade.

Most of the species in this chapter have developed a specific defense to combat a particular potentially lethal situation. Some tardigrades seem to have developed all those defenses, and several more besides. Depending on the threat, they may shut down into a dormant state, alter their metabolism to combat changing conditions, and perhaps use other strategies that scientists are still working to discover.

Here's an impressive—but incomplete—list of a few things that *won't* kill a tardigrade, but would reduce most other species (including ours) to dust: losing 97% of the water inside their bodies; being exposed to temperatures of 300 degrees or –450 degrees Fahrenheit; being stored at –320 degrees Fahrenheit for 20 months or –4 degrees Fahrenheit for 30 years; spending 10 days in the vacuum of space (including bare UV radiation from the sun); and straining under nearly 400 atmospheres of pressure. Whew!

Way to Go, Waterbear

Although many of the extreme conditions tardigrades have survived were cooked up (or frozen up, or rocketshipped up) by scientists, some tardigrades do enjoy life on the edge. Species have been found in extreme environments like Antarctica, the Sinai Desert, and the Himalayas.

If I Only Had a (Thawed) Brain

rctic ground squirrels are a lot like people who are too tough to admit when they're cold. You know the ones—you can see their bodies shivering and teeth chattering, but they still insist that they don't need you to turn up the heat, because they're perfectly toasty. These squirrels are so stubborn they actually break down their own brains just to prove that they can take the freeze.

Arctic ground squirrels live in Northern Canada and Siberia, and due to the extreme cold, they hibernate for 8 months of the year. Humans keep our internal body temperature around 98.6 degrees Fahrenheit, but during hibernation this squirrel can drop its temperature to 26 degrees, below the freezing point of water and the coldest known body temperature of any mammal. To prevent its blood from freezing, the squirrel uses a process called *supercooling*. For ice to form, it usually needs to attach to something called a "seed" molecule. The squirrel's blood eliminates as many of these molecules as possible, allowing the blood to drop below freezing without actually freezing solid. Even weirder, the squirrel's brain degenerates to conserve energy. Its brain cells shrink and some connections between the cells dissolve. In the warmer months, the brain regenerates itself and the connections grow back. Studying this squirrel's brain may one day help scientists develop new treatments for conditions like Alzheimer's disease, which causes severe memory loss in humans due to the death of brain cells and the connections between them.

Running Hot and Cold

Every 2–3 weeks during hibernation, the squirrel gets a bad case of the shivers, which warms its body up to its normal temperature. As soon as normal temperature is reached, it plunges it back down to freezing again. These quick warm-ups probably help the squirrel maintain its near-frozen state for long periods of time.

Giant sequoia   Lodgepole pines

Born From Fire

Few things are more dangerous and destructive than an uncontrolled fire. Lightning, volcanoes, and human carelessness can ignite a single spark that can destroy an entire habitat. In hot and dry regions, fires are quite common, but scientists have discovered that some plants have developed impressive fire tolerances that help them survive when they're feeling the burn.

Trees can be pretty thick-skinned, and by skin we mean bark. Many giant sequoias are thousands of years old, so they are built to outlast most of the things that try to kill them. Sequoia bark averages 8 to 10 inches thick, and can reach up to 2 feet in thickness. The bark is also a poor conductor of heat, which makes it an effective protection against forest fires (although a huge blaze will eventually take down these forest giants).

Other plants seem to revel in fire. Lodgepole pines mature their seeds in cones. Some cones remain shut—sometimes for 10–15 years—until a forest fire melts the resin

Fireweeds

Ponderosa pine

covering them, releasing the seeds so new trees can grow. Another plant has its love for fire right in its name. The seeds of the fireweed plant stay dormant in fire-prone areas. When a fire passes through, destroying most of the other vegetation, fireweeds seize the opportunity and sprout. With little competition from other plants, fireweeds grow quickly, reproduce, and their seeds fall to the ground, waiting patiently for the next big fire to come so they can sprout again.

Trial By Fire

The ponderosa pine is green at the top and thick and woody on the bottom, which gives the tree a survival advantage if a fire starts at the base. One estimate predicts that these trees can resist fire damage until more than half of the tree is consumed by flames.

Wood frog

Extreme Knowledge Trivia Answer

This animal can survive the winter months with 2/3 of the water in its body completely frozen.

    a.   **Wood frog (Correct)**

    b.   Snowshoe hare

    c.   Chinook salmon

Frog leg ice pops are a seasonal trend in the wild, because these amphibians actually survive being frozen solid. Their little bodies get so cold that they even stop breathing and their hearts stop beating—sometimes for weeks at a time. When the ice finally thaws, it's like an episode of The Croaking Dead coming to life.

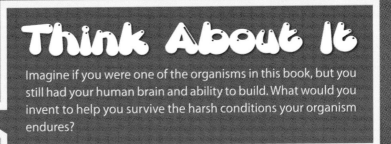

Think About It

Imagine if you were one of the organisms in this book, but you still had your human brain and ability to build. What would you invent to help you survive the harsh conditions your organism endures?

Dust mite

Bibliography

Chapter 1

There's No Place Like These Homes

Bordenstein, S. (n.d.). The Pompeii worm, Alvinella pompejana. *Marine Biological Laboratory.* Retrieved from http://serc.carleton.edu/microbelife/topics/marinesymbio sis/pompeii.html

Brooks, C. (2013). The life of extremophiles: Surviving in hostile habitats. *BBC Nature.* Retrieved from http://www.bbc.co.uk/nature/21923937

Bryner, J. (2014). Photos of the world's largest asphalt lake. *Live Science.* Retrieved from http://www.livescience.com/47237-largest-asphalt-lake-photos.html

Dickie, G. (2014). 5 animals that can take the extreme heat—and cold. *National Geographic.* Retrieved from http://voices.nationalgeographic.com/2014/07/30/ animals-science-extreme-temperatures-frozen-alaska-wood-frog

Geiling, N. (2016). The science behind Yellowstone's rainbow hot spring. *Smithsonian Magazine.* Retrieved from http://www.smithsonianmag.com/ist/?next=/travel/science-behind-yellowstones-rainbow-hot-spring-180950483

Keim, B. (2010). First animals found that live without oxygen. *WIRED.* Retrieved from http://www.wired.com/2010/04/anoxic-animals

Langston, J. (2015). Saharan silver ants use hair to survive Earth's hottest temperatures. *UW Today.* Retrieved from http://www.washington.edu/news/2015/06/18/saharan-silver-ants-use-hair-to-survive-earths-hottest-temperatures

Meckenstock, R., von Netzer, F., Stumpp, C., Lueders, T., Himmelberg, A., Hertkorn, N., . . . Schulze-Makuch, D. (2014). Water droplets in oil are microhabitats for microbial life. *Science, 345,* 673–676. http://dx.doi.org/10.1126/science.1252215

Mentel, M., & Martin, W. (2010). Anaerobic animals from an ancient, anoxic ecological niche. *BMC Biology, 8*(32). http://dx.doi.org/10.1186/1741-7007-8-32

MIT Technology Review. (2010). *Microbial life found in hydrocarbon lake.* Retrieved from https://www.technologyreview.com/s/418478/microbial-life-found-in-hydro carbon-lake

National Weather Service. (2016). *NWS windchill chart.* Retrieved from http://www.nws. noaa.gov/om/winter/windchill.shtml

Oskin, B. (2013). Deep-sea worms can't take the heat. *Live Science.* Retrieved from http:// www.livescience.com/34835-heat-limit-for-life.html

Phys.org. (2015). *Saharan silver ants can control electromagnetic waves over extremely broad spectrum range.* Retrieved from http://phys.org/news/2015-06-saharan-silver-ants-electromagnetic-extremely.html

Ravaux, J., Hamel, G., Zbinden, M., Tasiemski, A., Boutet, I., Léger, N., . . . Shillito, B. (2013). Thermal limit for Metazoan life in question: In vivo heat tolerance of the Pompeii worm. *Plos ONE, 8*(5), e64074. http://dx.doi.org/10.1371/journal.pone.0064074

Roach, J. (2004). Earth's hottest "bods" may belong to worms. *National Geographic.* Retrieved from http://news.nationalgeographic.com/news/2004/12/1208_041208_pompeii_worms.html

Roach, J. (2005). Hot-water worms may use bacteria as shield. *National Geographic.* Retrieved from http://news.nationalgeographic.com/news/2005/01/0117_050117_tubeworms.html

Schultz, C. (2013). In defense of the blobfish: Why the "world's ugliest animal" isn't as ugly as you think it is. *Smithsonian Magazine.* Retrieved from http://www.smithsonianmag. com/ist/?next=/smart-news/in-defense-of-the-blobfish-why-the-worlds-ugliest-animal-isnt-as-ugly-as-you-think-it-is-6676336

ScienceDaily. (2010). *First animals to live without oxygen discovered.* Retrieved from https:// www.sciencedaily.com/releases/2010/04/100407094450.htm

Sformo, T., Walters, K., Jeannet, K., Wowk, B., Fahy, G., Barnes, B., & Duman, J. (2010). Deep supercooling, vitrification and limited survival to -100 C in the Alaskan beetle Cucujus clavipes puniceus (Coleoptera: Cucujidae) larvae. *Journal of Experimental Biology, 213*, 502–509. http://dx.doi.org/10.1242/jeb.035758

Sokol, J. (2015). Silver coat lets Saharan ants withstand scorching desert heat. *New Scientist.* Retrieved from https://www.newscientist.com/article/dn27748-silver-coat-lets-saharan-ants-withstand-scorching-desert-heat

Vogel, G. (2010). ScienceShot: Animals that live without oxygen. *Science.* Retrieved from http://www.sciencemag.org/news/2010/04/scienceshot-animals-live-without-oxygen

Zastrow, M. (2014). Tiny water worlds float in oil reservoirs. *Nature.* Retrieved from http://www.nature.com/news/tiny-water-worlds-float-in-oil-reservoirs-1.15684

Chapter 2

Genes to the Extreme

American Lung Association. (2016). *Dust mites.* Retrieved from http://www.lung.org/our-initiatives/healthy-air/indoor/indoor-air-pollutants/dust-mites.html?referrer=https://www.google.com

Borrell, B. (2014). Why sharks have no bones. *Nature.* Retrieved from http://www.nature.com/news/why-sharks-have-no-bones-1.14487

Chen, X., Bracht, J., Goldman, A., Dolzhenko, E., Clay, D., Swart, E., . . . Landweber, L. (2014). The architecture of a scrambled genome reveals massive levels of genomic rearrangement during development. *Cell, 158,* 1187–1198. http://dx.doi.org/10.1016/j.cell.2014.07.034

Erickson, J. (2014). Sharing that crowded holiday flight with countless hitchhiking dust mites. *University of Michigan News.* Retrieved from http://www.ns.umich.edu/new/releases/22564-sharing-that-crowded-holiday-flight-with-countless-hitchhiking-dust-mites

Food and Agriculture Organization of the United Nations. (n.d.). *Banana varieties resistant to fungus are identified using mutation induction.* Retrieved from http://www.fao.org/in-action/banana-varieties-resistant-to-fungus-are-identified-using-mutation-induction/en

Giller, G. (2014). Slowly evolving elephant shark offers clues about why some fishes have no bones. *Scientific American.* Retrieved from http://www.scientificamerican.com/gallery/slowly-evolving-elephant-shark-offers-clues-about-why-some-fishes-have-no-bones

Ibarra-Laclette, E., Lyons, E., Hernández-Guzmán, G., Pérez-Torres, C., Carretero-Paulet, L., Chang, T., . . . Mockler, T. (2013). Architecture and evolution of a minute plant genome. *Nature, 498*(7452), 94–98. http://dx.doi.org/10.1038/nature12132

Kelly, M. (2014). In one of nature's innovations, a single cell smashes and rebuilds its own genome. *Princeton.edu.* Retrieved from https://www.princeton.edu/main/news/archive/S41/01/85G88/index.xml?section=topstories

Leushkin, E., Sutormin, R., Nabieva, E., Penin, A., Kondrashov, A., & Logacheva, M. (2013). The miniature genome of a carnivorous plant Genlisea aurea contains a low number of genes and short non-coding sequences. *BMC Genomics, 14*(1), 476. http://dx.doi.org/10.1186/1471-2164-14-476

LMU Munich. (2016). *Plants with pocket-sized genomes.* Retrieved from https://www.en.uni-muenchen.de/news/newsarchiv/2014/heubl_botanik.html

Ordonez, N., Seidl, M., Waalwijk, C., Drenth, A., Kilian, A., Thomma, B., . . . Kema, G. H. J. (2015). Worse comes to worst: Bananas and Panama disease—When plant and pathogen clones meet. *PLOS Pathogens, 11*(11), e1005197.

Phys.org. (2014). *Whole-genome sequencing of the elephant shark offers insights into bone disease and immunity in humans.* Retrieved from http://phys.org/news/2014-03-whole-genome-sequencing-elephant-shark-insights.html

Sayres, M. W. (2013). *Accessible research: A tiny bladderwort (that's a plant with little "bladders") genome.* Retrieved from http://pandasthumb.org/archives/2013/05/accessible-rese-1.html

Shafique, R., Klimov, P., Inam, M., Chaudhary, F., & OConnor, B. (2014). Group 1 allergen genes in two species of house dust mites, Dermatophagoides farinae and D. pteronyssinus (Acari: Pyroglyphidae): Direct sequencing, characterization and polymorphism. *PLOS One, 9*(12), e114636. http://dx.doi.org/10.1371/journal.pone.0114636

Sirucek, S. (2014). Two-faced cats: How do they get that way? *National Geographic.* Retrieved from http://news.nationalgeographic.com/news/2014/12/141205-janus-cat-two-faced-frank-louie-animals-science

Venkatesh, B., Lee, A., Ravi, V., Maurya, A., Lian, M., Swann, J., . . . Warren, W. (2014). Elephant shark genome provides unique insights into gnathostome evolution. *Nature, 505,* 174–179. http://dx.doi.org/10.1038/nature12826

Washington University in St Louis. (2014). Elephant shark genome decoded: New insights gained into bone formation and immunity. *ScienceDaily.* Retrieved from https://www.sciencedaily.com/releases/2014/01/140108133147.htm

Yong, E. (2013). You have 46 chromosomes. This pond creature has 15,600. *National Geographic.* Retrieved from http://phenomena.nationalgeographic.com/2013/02/06/you-have-46-chromsomes-this-pond-creature-has-15600

Chapter 3

Gross Anatomy

Botanical Society of America. (n.d.). *Hydnora africana.* Retrieved from http://botany.org/Parasitic_Plants/Hydnora_africana.php

Davies, E. (2011). Spiders use bubble webs 'like gills.' *BBC Nature.* Retrieved from http://www.bbc.co.uk/nature/13614742

de Pastino, B. (2006). Photo in the news: Bizarre assassin spiders discovered in Madagascar. *National Geographic.* Retrieved from http://news.nationalgeographic.com/news/2006/03/0308_060308_spider.html

Fungi3. (1st ed.). Retrieved from http://staff.washington.edu/raista/fungi3.pdf

Goldman, J. (2014). Four secrets your goldfish is hiding from you. *BBC.com.* Retrieved from http://www.bbc.com/earth/story/20141017-four-secrets-goldfish-are-hiding

Griffiths, S. (2013). The loneliest fish in the pond: Bubble-eyed goldfish has to swim on his own in case he bumps into others and BURSTS his eyes. *DailyMail.com.* Retrieved from http://www.dailymail.co.uk/sciencetech/article-2348775/Are-having-bubble-The-bonkers-eye-popping-goldfish-craze-sweeping-South-Africa.html

Jameson-Gould, J. (2012). *Hydnora africana.* Retrieved from http://www.realmonstrosities. com/2012/12/hydnora-africana.html

Law, Y. (2016). Why this caterpillar wears a hat made of discarded heads. *BBC.com.* Retrieved from http://www.bbc.com/earth/story/20160309-why-this-caterpillar-wears-a-hat-made-of-discarded-heads?ocid=fbert

Milius, S. (2014). Pelican spiders: Slow, safe assassins. *ScienceNews.* Retrieved from https://www.sciencenews.org/article/pelican-spiders-slow-safe-assassins

Ohnishi, K. (1993). Development of color vision in goldfish: selective delayed maturation of blue vision. *Elsevier, 33,* 1665–1672. doi:10.1016/0042-6989(93)90032-R

Sain, T. (n.d.). Hydnora Africana. *Our Breathing Planet.* Retrieved from http://www.ourbreathingplanet.com/hydnora-africana

Seymour, R., & Hetz, S. (2011). The diving bell and the spider: the physical gill of Argyroneta aquatica. *Journal of Experimental Biology, 214,* 2175–2181. http://dx.doi.org/10.1242/jeb.056093

Simon, M. (2014). Absurd creature of the week: The world's goofiest-looking spider is actually a brutal ninja. *WIRED.* Retrieved from http://www.wired.com/2014/12/absurd-creature-of-the-week-assassin-spider

Universities Federation for Animal Welfare. (n.d.). *Bubble-eye goldfish.* Retrieved from http://www.ufaw.org.uk/fish/bubble-eye-goldfish-bubble-eye

Yong, E. (2016). This caterpillar builds a protective hat from old heads. *National Geographic.* Retrieved from http://phenomena.nationalgeographic.com/2016/03/03/this-caterpillar-builds-a-protective-hat-from-old-heads

Zahl, P. (2009). Bubble eye goldfish, United States. *National Geographic.* Retrieved from http://photography.nationalgeographic.com/photography/photo-of-the-day/goldfish-zahl

Zheng, C., Sohn, M., & Kim, W. (2006). Atromentin and Leucomelone, the first inhibitors specific to enoyl-ACP reductase (FabK) of Streptococcus pneumoniae. *The Journal of Antiobiotics, 59,* 808–812. http://dx.doi.org/10.1038/ja.2006.108

Chapter 4
Supersize Species

Atlas Obscura. (n.d.). *Pando, the trembling giant*. Retrieved from http://www.atlasobscura.com/places/pando-the-trembling-giant

Birmingham Zoo. (n.d.). *Kori Bustard*. Retrieved from https://www.birminghamzoo.com/animal/kori-bustard

Casselman, A. (2007). Strange but true: The largest organism on Earth is a fungus. *Scientific American*. Retrieved from http://www.scientificamerican.com/article/strange-but-true-largest-organism-is-fungus

Crew, B. (2012). Lord Howe Island stick insects are going home. *Scientific American*. Retrieved from http://blogs.scientificamerican.com/running-ponies/lord-howe-island-stick-insects-are-going-home

Fleming, N. (2014). The largest living thing on Earth is a humongous fungus. *BBC.com*. Retrieved from http://www.bbc.com/earth/story/20141114-the-biggest-organism-in-the-world

Franklin Park Zoo. (n.d.). *Kori Bustard*. Retrieved from http://www.zoonewengland.org/franklin-park-zoo/our-animals/birds/kori-bustard

Grant, M. (1993). The trembling giant. *Discover*. Retrieved from http://discovermagazine.com/1993/oct/thetremblinggian285

Illinois Department of Public Health. (n.d.). *Biting flies*. Retrieved from http://www.idph.state.il.us/envhealth/pcbitingflies.htm

Jabr, F. (2012). How brainless slime molds redefine intelligence [Video file]. *Scientific American*. Retrieved from http://www.scientificamerican.com/article/brainless-slime-molds

Japanese spider crab. (n.d.). Retrieved from http://mkm5056.cias.rit.edu/giants/spicrab.html

Krulwich, R. (2012). Six-legged giant finds secret hideaway, hides for 80 years. *NPR*. Retrieved from http://www.npr.org/sections/krulwich/2012/02/24/147367644/six-legged-giant-finds-secret-hideaway-hides-for-80-years

Li, Z. (2014). World's largest aquatic insect specimen found in China. *CNN*. Retrieved from http://www.cnn.com/2014/07/22/world/asia/giant-insect-china

Marshall, M. (2015). Mydas flies and timber flies are the biggest flies. *BBC.com*. Retrieved from http://www.bbc.com/earth/story/20150614-the-biggest-flies-in-the-world

McDonnell Genome Institute. (n.d.). *Genome: Physarum polycephalum*. Retrieved from http://genome.wustl.edu/genomes/detail/physarum-polycephalum

NaturePlus. (2015). Big is beautiful in the world of flies. *Natural History Museum*. Retrieved from http://www.nhm.ac.uk/natureplus/blogs/diptera-blog/2015/06/08/big-is-beautiful-in-the-world-of-flies?fromGateway=true

Okamoto, K. (2001). Limb loss in the giant spider crab Macrocheira kaempferi. *Bulletin of the Shizuoka Prefectural Fisheries Experiment Station (Japan)*. Retrieved from http://agris.fao.org/agris-search/search.do?recordID=JP2003000209

Owen, J. (2015). World's biggest fly faces two new challengers. *National Geographic*. Retrieved from http://news.nationalgeographic.com/2015/12/151210-biggest-animals-science-insects-flies-new-species

Parr, C. (n.d.). Physarum polycephalum: Many-headed slime. *Encyclopedia of Life*. Retrieved from http://eol.org/pages/1002810/overview

Riebel, W. (n.d.). Macrocheira kaempferi. *Animal Diversity Web*. Retrieved from http://animaldiversity.org/accounts/Macrocheira_kaempferi

SciTech Daily. (2013). *Brainless slime mold Physarum polycephalum shows intelligence*. Retrieved from http://scitechdaily.com/brainless-slime-mold-physarum-polycephalum-shows-intelligence

Smithsonian Ocean Portal. (n.d.). *Japanese spider crab*. Retrieved from http://ocean.si.edu/ocean-photos/japanese-spider-crab

Tennessee Aquarium. (n.d.). *Giant Japanese spider crab*. Retrieved from http://www.tnaqua.org/our-animals/invertebrates/giant-japanese-spider-crab

Tu, C. (2015). Earth's biggest living thing might be a tree with thousands of clones. *Public Radio International*. Retrieved from http://www.pri.org/stories/2015-05-05/earths-biggest-living-thing-might-be-tree-thousands-clones

U.S. National Park Service. (n.d.). *Quaking Aspen*. Retrieved from https://www.nps.gov/brca/learn/nature/quakingaspen.htm

University of California Museum of Paleontology. (n.d.). *Introduction to the "slime molds."* Retrieved from http://www.ucmp.berkeley.edu/protista/slimemolds.html

Woods Hole Oceanographic Institution. (2000). *The world's largest bacteria.* Retrieved from https://www.whoi.edu/page.do?pid=14958&tid=7342&cid=46727

Zoos Victoria. (2016). *13,000 and counting.* Retrieved from http://www.zoo.org.au/news/13000-and-counting

Chapter 5

Eat, Drink, and Be Scary

Carter, J., Hyland, C., Steele, R., & Collins, E. (2016). Dynamics of mouth opening in Hydra. *Biophysical Journal, 110,* 1191–1201. http://dx.doi.org/10.1016/j.bpj.2016.01.008

Daley, J. (2016). How Hydra rip open new mouths at every meal. *Smithsonian Magazine.* Retrieved from http://www.smithsonianmag.com/smart-news/how-hydra-rip-open-new-mouths-every-meal-180958372/?utm_source=facebook.com&no-ist

Davies, E. (2012). Bone-eating worms drill with acid. *BBC.com.* Retrieved from http://www.bbc.co.uk/nature/18594493

EDGE. (n.d.). *Olm (Proteus anguinus).* Retrieved from http://www.edgeofexistence.org/amphibians/species_info.php?id=563

Encyclopedia Britannica. (n.d.). *Shrike.* Retrieved from http://www.britannica.com/animal/shrike

Ghose, T. (2014). Six mysterious blood-sucking ant species discovered in Madagascar. *Live Science.* Retrieved from http://www.livescience.com/44479-new-dracula-ant-species.html

Goodman, S. (2000). The strange world of the shrike. *National Wildlife Federation.* Retrieved from https://www.nwf.org/News-and-Magazines/National-Wildlife/Birds/Archives/2000/The-Strange-World-of-the-Shrike.aspx

Griggs, M. B. (2015). Bone eating 'zombie' worm has been around for 100 million years. *Popular Science.* Retrieved from http://www.popsci.com/bone-eating-zombie-worm-has-been-around-100-million-years

Inglis-Arkell, E. (2015). This animal can go over a decade without food. *Io9.* Retrieved from http://io9.gizmodo.com/this-animal-can-go-over-a-decade-without-food-172330
4968

Jameson-Gould, J. (2011). *Olm.* Retrieved from http://www.realmonstrosities.com/2011/02/olm.html

Kaplan, M. (2009). "Surreal" vegetarian spider found—A first. *National Geographic.* Retrieved from http://news.nationalgeographic.com/news/2009/10/091012-vegetarian-spider.html

Kiel, S., Goedert, J., Kahl, W., & Rouse, G. (2010). Fossil traces of the bone-eating worm Osedax in early Oligocene whale bones. *Proceedings of the National Academy of Sciences, 107,* 8656–8659. http://dx.doi.org/10.1073/pnas.1002014107

Michigan State University. (n.d.). *Jumping spider.* Retrieved from http://www.pestid.msu.edu/insects-and-arthropods/jumping-spider

Monterey Bay Aquarium. (n.d.). *Whale worm.* Retrieved from http://www.montereybayaquarium.org/animal-guide/invertebrates/whale-worm

National Geographic. (n.d.). *World's weirdest: Cute bird impales its prey* [Video file]. Retrieved from http://video.nationalgeographic.com/video/weirdest-shrike

Nuwer, R. (2013). How bone-eating zombie worms drill through whale skeletons. *Smithsonian Magazine.* Retrieved from http://www.smithsonianmag.com/smart-news/how-bone-eating-zombie-worms-drill-through-whale-skeletons-46666314

Pappas, S. (2016). These spiders like some greens with their insects. *Live Science.* Retrieved from http://www.livescience.com/54054-plant-eating-spiders-revealed.html

Perlman, D. (2001). Discovery of blood-sucking ant species scrambles some theories. *SFGate.* Retrieved from http://www.sfgate.com/news/article/Discovery-of-Blood-Sucking-Ant-Species-Scrambles-2964755.php

Rogers, K. (2016). Bagheera kiplingi. *Encyclopedia Britannica.* Retrieved from http://www.britannica.com/animal/Bagheera-kiplingi

Smithsonian Ocean Portal. (n.d.). *Zombie worms crave bone*. Retrieved from http://ocean.si.edu/ocean-news/zombie-worms-crave-bone

Susan. (2011). *The Olm—Earth's weirdest salamander*. Retrieved from http://frogsaregreen.org/the-olm-earths-weirdest-salamander

What will we discover today? The Dracula ant. (2010). Retrieved from http://asbiomed.com/blog/?p=196

Wildscreen Arkive. (n.d.). *Dracula ant (Adetomyrma venatrix)*. Retrieved from http://www.arkive.org/dracula-ant/adetomyrma-venatrix

Yong, E. (2010). The olm: the blind cave salamander that lives to 100. *Discover*. Retrieved from http://blogs.discovermagazine.com/notrocketscience/2010/07/20/the-olm-the-blind-cave-salamander-that-lives-to-100/#.VzQFSYQrKCg

Yosef, R., & Whitman, D. (1992). Predator exaptations and defensive adaptations in evolutionary balance: No defence is perfect. *Evolutionary Ecology, 6*, 527–536. http://dx.doi.org/10.1007/bf02270696

Chapter 6

Death Defiers

American Journal of Botany. (2011). How lodgepole pines protect their kind against fire, mountain pine beetles infestation. *Science Daily*. Retrieved from https://www.sciencedaily.com/releases/2011/05/110531155402.htm

American Museum of Natural History. (2015). *The immortal jellyfish*. Retrieved from http://www.amnh.org/explore/news-blogs/on-exhibit-posts/the-immortal-jellyfish

Biology Pop. (2014). *Turritopsis dohrnii "the immortal jellyfish."* Retrieved from http://biologypop.com/turritopsis-dohrnii-the-immortal-jellyfish

Charron, A., & Quatrano, R. (2009). Between a rock and a dry place: The water-stressed moss. *Molecular Plant, 2*, 478–486. http://dx.doi.org/10.1093/mp/ssp018

Costanzo, J., do Amaral, M., Rosendale, A., & Lee, R. (2013). Hibernation physiology, freezing adaptation and extreme freeze tolerance in a northern population of the wood frog. *Journal of Experimental Biology, 216,* 3461–3473. http://dx.doi.org/10.1242/jeb.089342

Gough, Z. (2015). Arctic ground squirrels' supercool slumber. *BBC.com.* Retrieved from http://www.bbc.com/earth/story/20150218-arctic-ground-squirrels-supercool-slumber

Griggs, M. B. (2015). A tree that could stop wildfires. *Popular Science.* Retrieved from http://www.popsci.com/cypress-trees-are-resistant-to-wildfires

The immortal jellyfish. (n.d.). Retrieved from http://immortal-jellyfish.com

Jabr, F. (2012). What the supercool arctic ground squirrel teaches us about the brain's resilience. *Scientific American.* Retrieved from http://www.scientificamerican.com/article/arctic-ground-squirrel-brain

McDermott, M. (2014). 5 reasons why the tardigrade is nature's toughest animal. *National Geographic.* Retrieved from http://tvblogs.nationalgeographic.com/2014/03/19/5-reasons-why-the-tardigrade-is-natures-toughest-animal

Miller, W. (2011). Tardigrades. *American Scientist.* Retrieved from http://www.americanscientist.org/issues/feature/tardigrades/99999

Oliver, M. (1991). Influence of protoplasmic water loss on the control of protein synthesis in the desiccation-tolerant moss Tortula ruralis: Ramifications for a repair-based mechanism of desiccation tolerance. *Plant Physiology, 97,* 1501–1511. Retrieved from http://www.ncbi.nlm.nih.gov/pmc/articles/PMC1081193

Petruzzello, M. (n.d.). Playing with wildfire: 5 amazing adaptations of pyrophytic plants. *Encyclopedia Britannica.* Retrieved from http://www.britannica.com/list/5-amazing-adaptations-of-pyrophytic-plants

Pyne, S. (n.d.). How plants use fire (and are used by it). *PBS.* Retrieved from http://www.pbs.org/wgbh/nova/fire/plants.html

Quammen, D. (2012). Sequoias: Scaling a forest giant. *National Geographic.* Retrieved from http://ngm.nationalgeographic.com/2012/12/sequoias/quammen-text

Quirós, G. (2015). These 'resurrection plants' spring back to life in seconds. *KQED Science.* Retrieved from http://ww2.kqed.org/science/2015/06/25/these-resurrection-plants-spring-back-to-life-in-seconds

Reardon, S. (2013). Zoologger: Supercool squirrels go into the deep freeze. *New Scientist.* Retrieved from https://www.newscientist.com/article/dn23107-zoologger-supercool-squirrels-go-into-the-deep-freeze

Rocca, G., Hernando, C., Madrigal, J., Danti, R., Moya, J., Guijarro, M., . . . Moya, B. (2015). Possible land management uses of common cypress to reduce wildfire initiation risk: A laboratory study. *Journal of Environmental Management, 159,* 68–77. doi:10.1016/j.jenvman.2015.05.020

Scharping, N. (2016). Tardigrades, frozen for 30 years, spring back to life. *Discover.* Retrieved from http://blogs.discovermagazine.com/d-brief/2016/01/18/frozen-for-30-years-a-tardigrade-springs-back-to-life/#.VyrVWVaDGko

Schonbeck, M., & Bewley, J. (1981). Responses of the moss Tortula ruralis to desiccation treatments. I. Effects of minimum water content and rates of dehydration and rehydration. *Canadian Journal of Botany, 59,* 2698–2706. doi:10.1139/b81-320

Simon, M. (2014). Absurd creature of the week: The incredible critter that's tough enough to survive in space. *WIRED.* Retrieved from http://www.wired.com/2014/03/absurd-creature-week-water-bear

Sirucek, S. (2013). How Arctic frogs survive being frozen alive. *National Geographic.* Retrieved from http://voices.nationalgeographic.com/2013/08/21/how-the-alaska-wood-frog-survives-being-frozen

Than, K. (2009). "Immortal" jellyfish swarm world's oceans. *National Geographic.* Retrieved from http://news.nationalgeographic.com/news/2009/01/090130-immortal-jellyfish-swarm.html

Tsujimoto, M., Imura, S., & Kanda, H. (2016). Recovery and reproduction of an Antarctic tardigrade retrieved from a moss sample frozen for over 30 years. *Cryobiology 72*(1), 78–81. Retrieved from http://www.sciencedirect.com/science/article/pii/S0011224015300134

U.S. National Park Service. (n.d.). *The giant sequoia of the Sierra Nevada (Chapter 2).* Retrieved from https://www.nps.gov/parkhistory/online_books/science/hartesveldt/chap2.htm

U.S. National Park Service. (n.d.). *Lodgepole pine.* Retrieved from https://www.nps.gov/yell/learn/nature/lodgepole.htm

U.S. National Park Service. (n.d.). *Trees—Ponderosa pine*. Retrieved from https://www.nps.gov/wica/learn/nature/trees-ponderosa-pine.htm

U.S. National Park Service. (2016). *Jack pine: Great Lakes states*. Retrieved from https://www.nps.gov/fire/wildland-fire/learning-center/fire-in-depth/different-ecosystems/jack-pine-greatlakes.cfm

von der Ohe, C., Darian-Smith, C., Garner, C., & Heller, H. (2006). Ubiquitous and temperature-dependent neural plasticity in hibernators. *Journal of Neuroscience, 26,* 10590–10598. http://dx.doi.org/10.1523/jneurosci.2874-06.2006

Image Credits

The publisher would like to thank the following for their permission to reproduce their images:

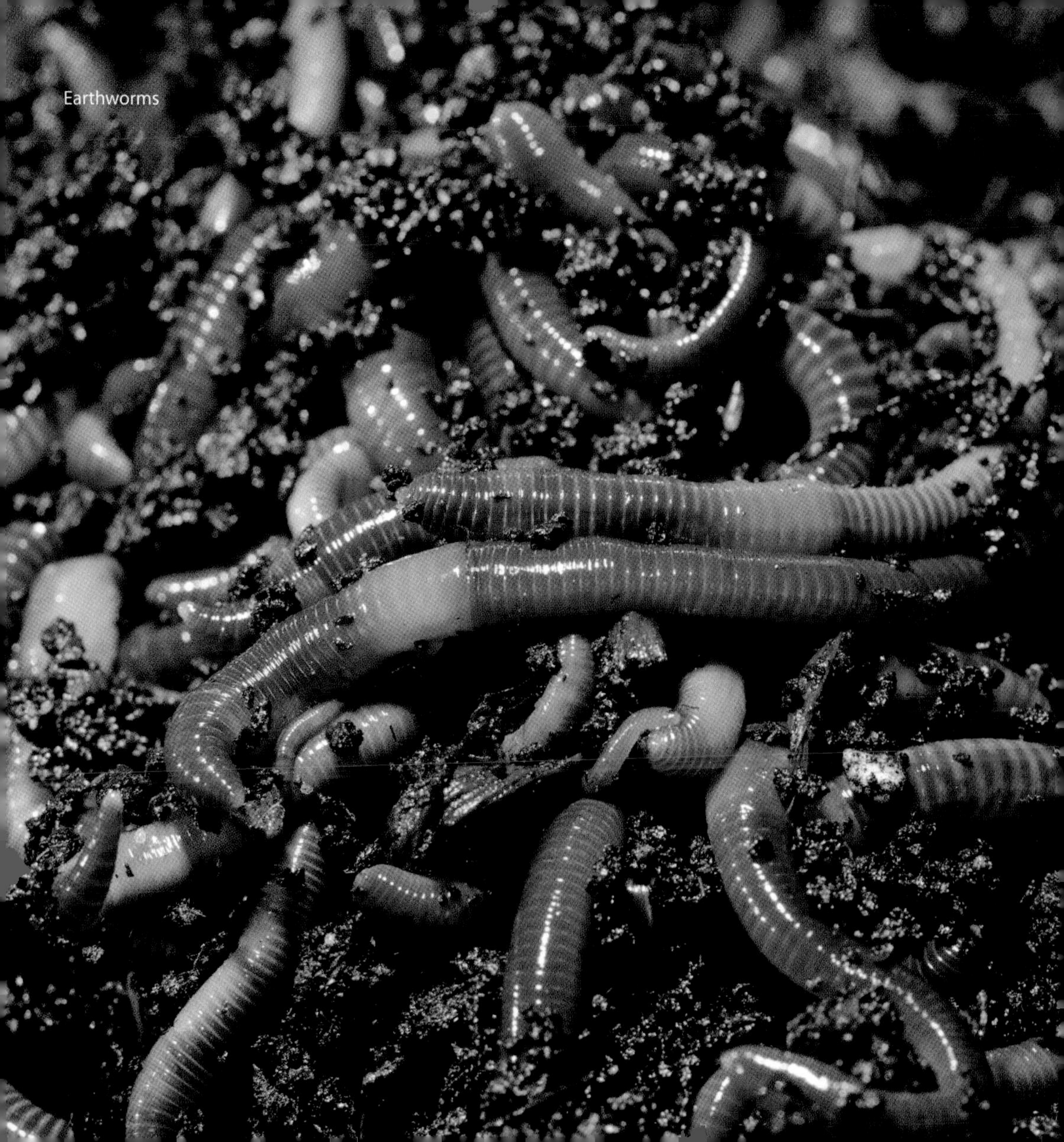
Earthworms

About
the Authors

Jenn and Charlie are Boston-based science nerds who met through stand-up comedy. By day, Jenn writes science textbooks and Charlie slings data for a cancer research company. By night, they make comedy films and stay up past their bedtime e-mailing pictures of weird animals to each other.